TIM JEFFS ART
Animal Sketches
AFRICAN
Wildlife

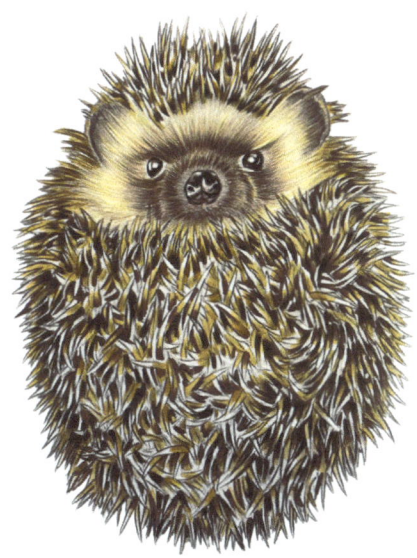

ANIMALS OF THE WORLD Coloring Book Series

For Jane, Jenna and Harrison

Dedicated to all of the wonderful colorists who have supported my art and made my drawings more beautiful with their colors, and all the precious creatures that we live among. A special thank you to Jo Warren for all of her continued support and beautiful colorings and lesson that make this book so much more special! And to my niece Meagan Jeffs-Rossouw, whose wonderful introduction about her time living with her family in Africa sheds a shining light on Africa and its precious wildlife.

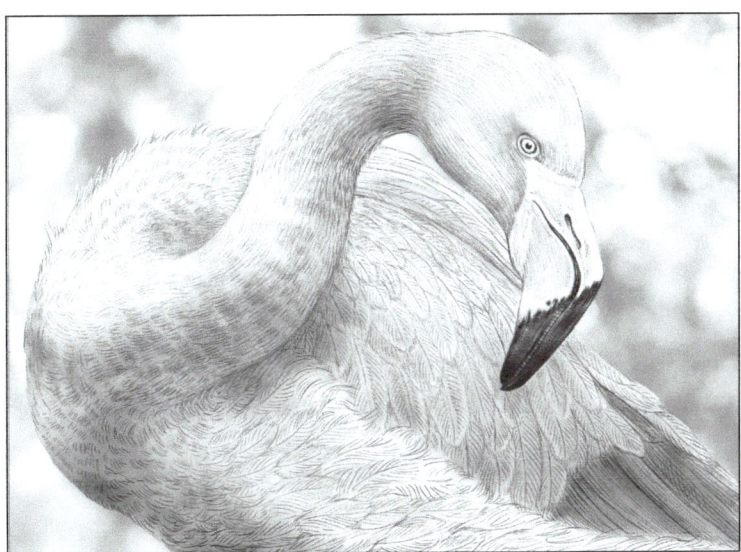 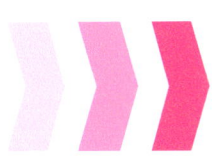 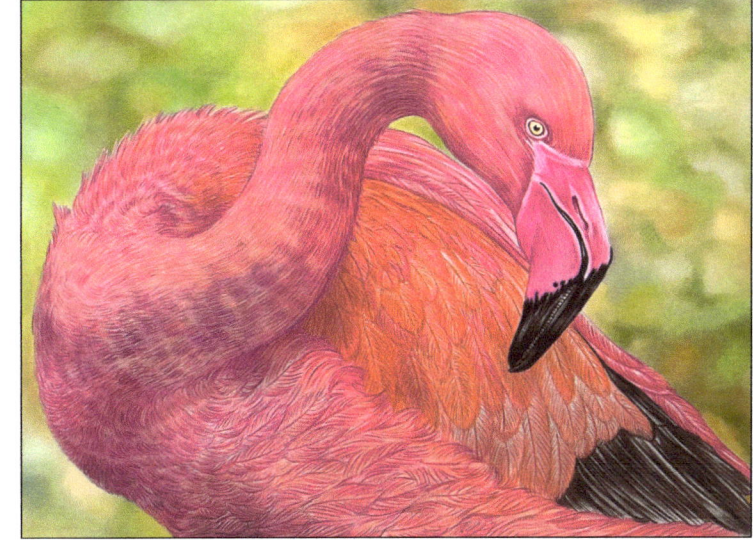

Grayscale coloring page before... ...and after you bring it to life with your colorful imagination!

© Copyright 2021 Tim Jeffs Art
All rights reserved. No part of this publication may be reproduced or distributed in any form without the prior written permission of Tim Jeffs Art.

Tim Jeffs Art
376 East Madison Avenue, Dumont, NJ 07628

AFRICAN Wildlife Thoughts

Africa Through My Families Eyes

I dream of going on an African Safari one day to experience Africa's animals as they should be, in the wild. But until then I have a very cherished connection to the wildlife in Africa. My niece Meagan Jeffs-Rossouw and her husband Marius and son Ryan lived in Kenya for years. Marius grew up in Zimbabwe and Ryan was born in Kenya. The stories and pictures from their travels throughout Africa have been such an inspiration to all my African Wildlife drawings. I thought it would be very special to let her explain to you her families personal story of living amongst Africa's wondrous wildlife.

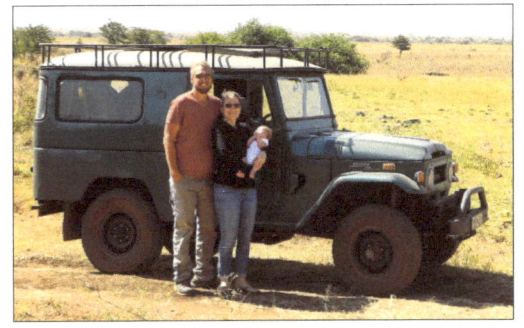

Marius, Meagan and Ryan in the African Bush.

Meagan's Africa Story

My husband, my son and I have been fortunate enough to be able to experience first hand the breathtaking wild spaces and wildlife that exist uniquely throughout the continent of Africa. Imagine living in a place where the animals in this book are not just pages in which you are about to color… but animals that you may interact with in your regular day to day life! This is the reality for many people all around Africa.

Life in Kenya was different for us in many ways… but what sticks out the most was having interactions with wildlife every single day, big or small, welcomed or not. We had resident geckos in our house and could step outside our front door and find gorgeous chameleons in our garden. We learned not to leave any windows open if we left the house because monkeys could invite themselves in and help themselves to everything in our kitchen. Sometimes we would get alerts on our phones letting us know that the lions have left the neighboring Nairobi National Park and were roaming around the neighborhood (and to make sure that all small pets were brought inside)! We were able to visit our baby elephant friends at the elephant orphanage just down the road. And I loved feeding the giraffes and getting kisses from them and then going for a walk in the nature park that was a part of the Giraffe Center just around the corner from us. Our dear friend there was known for rehabilitating all kinds of little creatures and birds. She once asked me to help with a hypothermic and severely dehydrated hedgehog that was found in the middle of the road. So we converted our bathroom into its temporary home while I helped nurse it back to health before releasing it again. What I miss the most is going on camping safaris… being out in the bush for extended periods of time, sometimes not seeing another human for days. There is nothing that makes me feel more at peace and happier than being

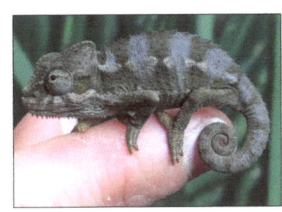

Chameleon in the garden.

Rehabilitating a dehydrated hedgehog

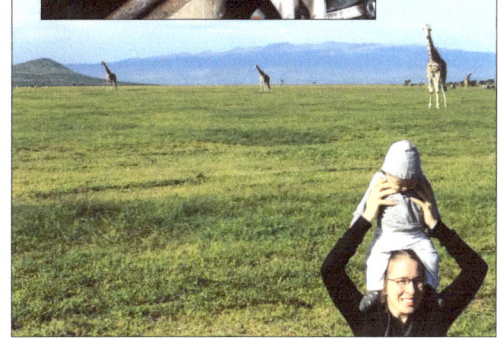

Getting a Giraffe kiss, Ryan with an orphaned elephant at the Sheldrick Wildlife Trust, and Meagan and Ryan in the bush with Giraffes.

out in the bush, taking in all that there is in the surrounding environment, all the sights, smells and sounds. Just imagine being close enough to be able to feel the vibrations from elephants communicating to each other with their deep rumbling, throaty sounds in the middle of the night while camping in the bush. Nothing but the thin nylon fabric separating you from these gentle giants…to me, nothing is more exhilarating! Or witnessing the unforgettable sights and sounds of thousands of animals during the Great Migration that happens between Tanzania and Kenya every year.

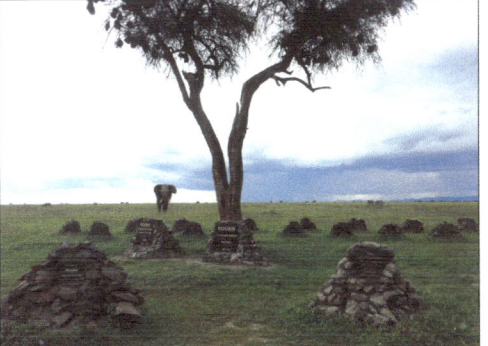

The rhino graveyard in Ol' Pajeta Conservancy, Kenya. The resting place of the last male Northern White Rhinoceros.

These are some of our never-to-be-forgotten treasured moments. I want nothing more than to be able to assure that similar profound experiences will continue to be available to my children and to future generations.

Nature is all around us, but society has conditioned us to believe that we are separate and different from nature. The consumer culture that we are all a part of has really minimized just how special wildlife and wild spaces truly are. Oftentimes we see an amazing nature photograph on social media and think "oh wow, that's beautiful!" for… maybe half a second before swiping on to the next image. When we disconnect ourselves from the hustle and bustle and put our devices down to go be outside, life slows down a bit and you can develop a real appreciation for how much more there is to that particular moment. You have the time to observe all the details… how everything moves and interacts with each other and with the environment all around you. This coloring book that Tim has created took time to create. He studied each animal and then captured some of the most intricate details that make each of these animals so very special. Not everyone has the opportunity to see African wildlife in person in their natural habitats, but I hope that your time spent coloring in the details of these majestic animals will help you to slow down and connect with them and inspire you to take actions to ensure their survival for generations to come. Conservation doesn't just happen… we have to do our part and learn to live together.

Coloring Thoughts

In this coloring book I've drawn the animals on various backgrounds. Some of the animals I've drawn in their natural environments, some on black backgrounds to enhance your colors and make them pop. I hope this will give you further coloring creativity options to have fun with. I hope you enjoy coloring this group of African animals as much as I enjoyed drawing them, and I know that with your colors, you will bring these beautiful African animals to life!

Photographs ©
Meagan Jeffs-Rossouw and
Marius Rossouw

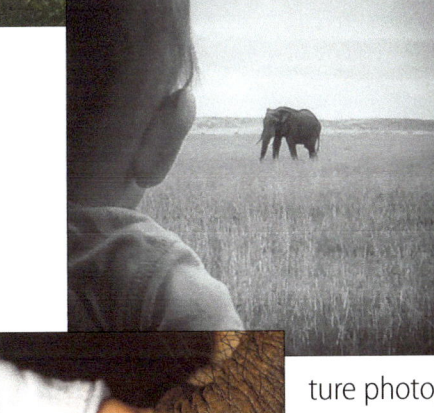

Ryan's African Wildlife connection.

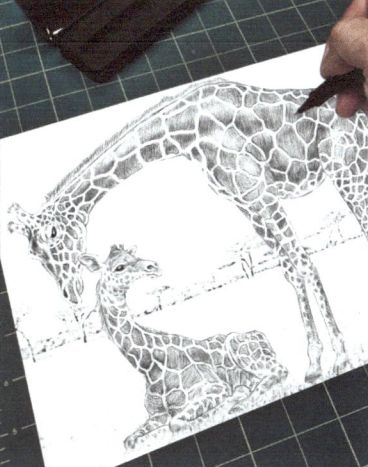

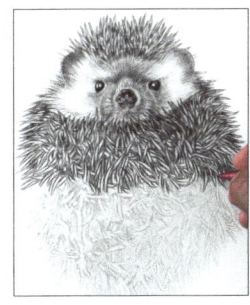

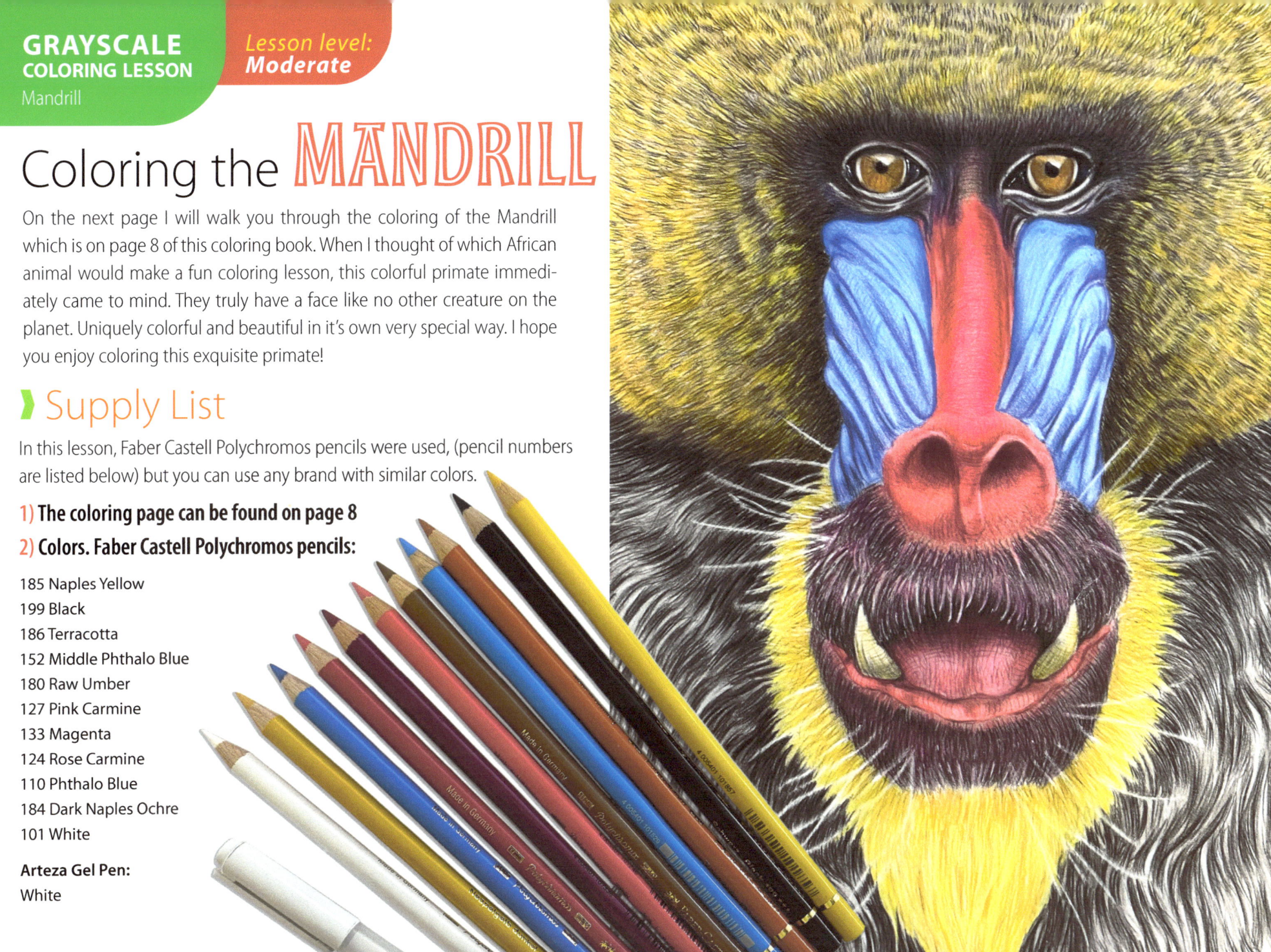

GRAYSCALE COLORING LESSON
Mandrill

Lesson level: Moderate

Coloring the MANDRILL

On the next page I will walk you through the coloring of the Mandrill which is on page 8 of this coloring book. When I thought of which African animal would make a fun coloring lesson, this colorful primate immediately came to mind. They truly have a face like no other creature on the planet. Uniquely colorful and beautiful in it's own very special way. I hope you enjoy coloring this exquisite primate!

❯ Supply List

In this lesson, Faber Castell Polychromos pencils were used, (pencil numbers are listed below) but you can use any brand with similar colors.

1) **The coloring page can be found on page 8**
2) **Colors. Faber Castell Polychromos pencils:**

185 Naples Yellow
199 Black
186 Terracotta
152 Middle Phthalo Blue
180 Raw Umber
127 Pink Carmine
133 Magenta
124 Rose Carmine
110 Phthalo Blue
184 Dark Naples Ochre
101 White

Arteza Gel Pen:
White

GRAYSCALE COLORING LESSON
Mandrill

MANDRILL
Making your Mandrill come to life with color

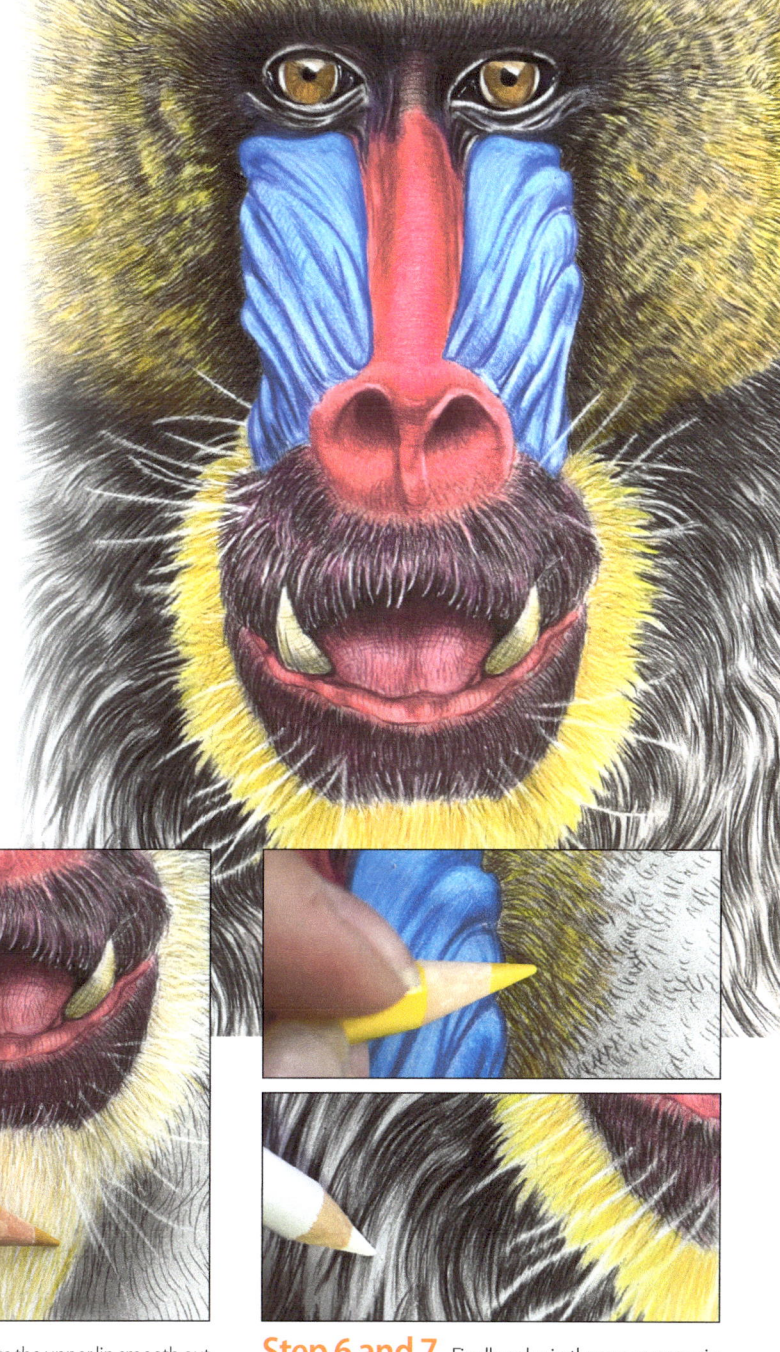

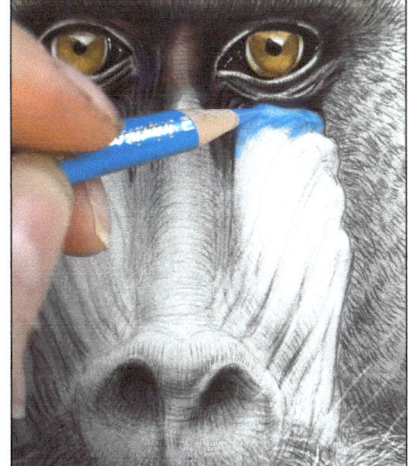

Step 1. Start by coloring in the eyes with Naples Yellow and blend Terracotta over the darker areas of the eye balls. Shade in the eye sockets and eye brow using Black and Magenta. Using Middle Phthalo Blue put down a first layer on the muzzle.

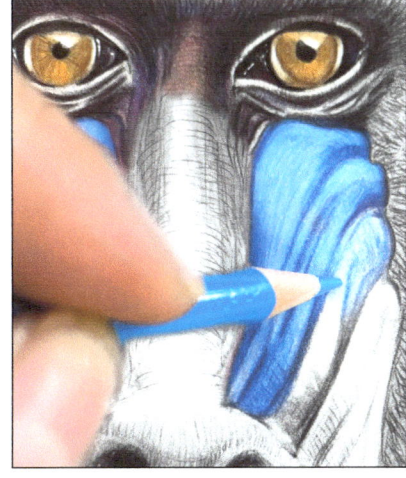

Step 2. To create a 3D effect on the blue muzzle shade in the edges of each section with Phthalo Blue. This will create depth and separate the section from one another. Finish the lighter areas by blending over them with a layer of white.

You did it! Your Mandrill has come to life with color!

Coloring Steps by Jo Warren

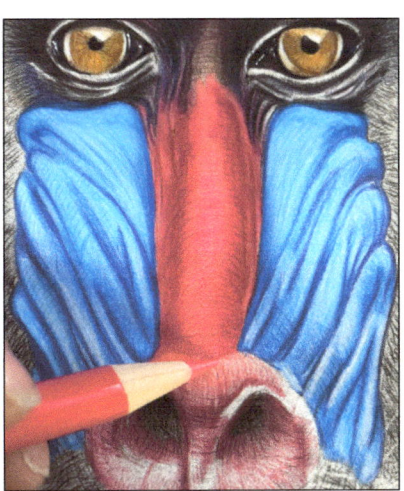

Step 3. For the nose first color a base coat using white. Next color a layer using Pink Carmine followed by Rose Carmine for the darker areas. End by finishing the lighter areas again with white.

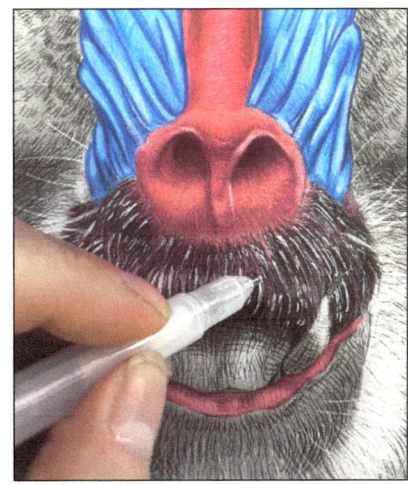

Step 4. After coloring in the upper lip with Magenta make the whiskers on the Mandrill's face more realistic using strokes of the white gel pen and then strokes with Black.

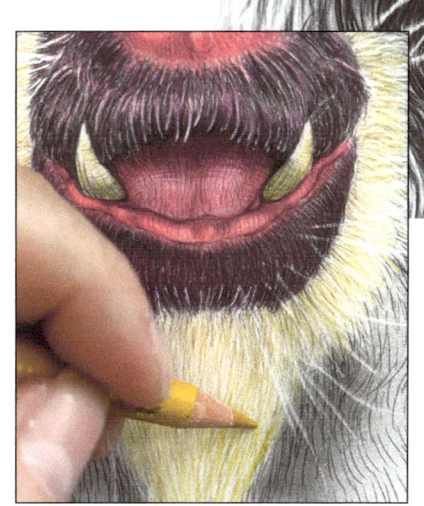

Step 5. To complete the upper lip smooth out and soften the white gel pen strokes using Magenta. Color in the chin hairs using Naples Yellow and layering strokes of Dark Naples Ochre on top.

Step 6 and 7. Finally color in the upper mane in short strokes using Naples Yellow, Raw Umber and Black. And color the lower mane using black and white. Blend the white over the black line to create gray flowing hair.

Learn About AFRICAN Wildlife

Before you start coloring, it's important to learn about the animals in this book and their conservation status.
And after you finish a coloring share your work on social media to help raise awareness about the animals conservation status.

❯ African Bush Elephants The largest living terrestrial animals reaching 13 feet in height and weighing up to 13,000 pounds. They live in core family units stretching across 37 African countries.
Conservation Status: Endangered

❯ African Pygmy Hedgehog Also known as the Four-Toed Hedgehog they are between 5-12 inches in length. They are nocturnal animals and their backs are covered with spikes for defense.
Conservation Status: Least Concern

❯ African Wild Dogs The largest wild canine in Africa they are highly social and live in packs of 2-27 adults. They are threatened by habitat fragmentation and disease.
Conservation Status: Endangered

❯ Giraffes The the tallest living terrestrial animal, there are 9 subspecies of Giraffe. They grow to 18 feet tall and weigh up to 2600 pounds. While sprinting they can reach speeds up to 37 miles per hour. They are threatened by hunting and habitat destruction.
Conservation Status: Vulnerable

❯ Greater Flamingo The most widespread flamingo it is found in Africa, India, the Middle East and Southern Europe. It is the largest living species of Flamingo and up to 60 inches tall. It's population is healthy.
Conservation Status: Least Concern

❯ Hooded Vulture Native to Sub-Saharan Africa it is found across Southern, Eastern and West Africa. It has become endangered due to hunting and habitat loss.
Conservation Status: Critically Endangered

❯ Lions A large wild cat that inhabits grasslands and Savannas through Africa Lions are very social animals and live in prides. Males can grow up to 500 pounds and females to 300 pounds. Estimated population is between 16-47,000 living in the wild in 2004.
Conservation Status: Vulnerable

❯ Mandrill Found in the tropical rainforests of Western Africa Mandrills are the world's largest monkey. They have a colorful face, long canines and can weigh up to 82 pounds. They are threatened by deforestation and hunting.
Conservation Status: Vulnerable

❯ Mountain Gorillas Found only in two isolated groups in East-Central Africa in high altitude bamboo forests there are estimated to only be 1063 left in the wild.
Conservation Status: Endangered

❯ Northern White Rhinoceros Formerly found in East and Central Africa there are only two known left alive today. Both are females thus sadly making the future of this beautiful creature extinct.
Conservation Status: Critically Endangered

❯ Red-Billed Hornbill Living in the savannas and woodlands of Sub-Saharan Africa this large bird can grow up to 17 inches in length. Their population is strong.
Conservation Status: Least Concern

❯ Sable Antelope Lives in wooded savanna in Eastern and Southern Africa. They grow to be 518 pounds and their horns can grow up to 65 inches long. Their population is stable.
Conservation Status: Least Concern

❯ Warthog Also know as Phacochoerus these pigs have large tusks and live in grasslands, savannas, and woodlands throughout sub-Saharan Africa.
Conservation Status: Least Concern

❯ Wildebeest Native to Eastern and Southern Africa these antelopes live in large herds and perform an annual migration in which 1.5 million animals move to new grazing grounds.
Conservation Status: Least Concern

❯ Zebra An African equine these black and white striped animals inhabit eastern and southern Africa and live alone or loosely associated herds. They are threatened due to hunting and habitat loss due to farming.
Conservation Status: Near Threatened

AFRICAN Wildlife Index

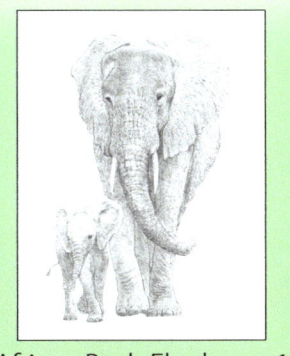
African Bush Elephants 1

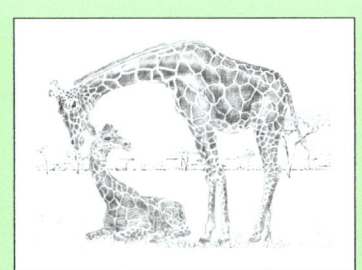
Giraffes 4

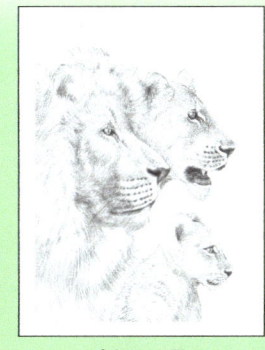
Lions 7

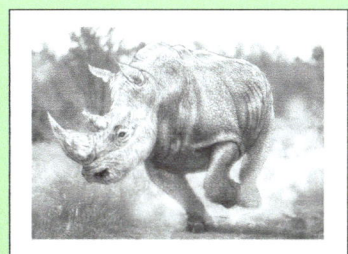
Northern White Rhinoceros 10

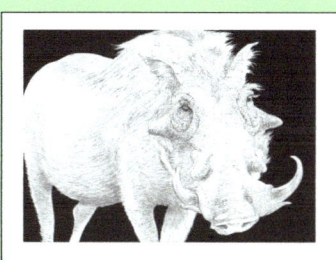
Warthog 13

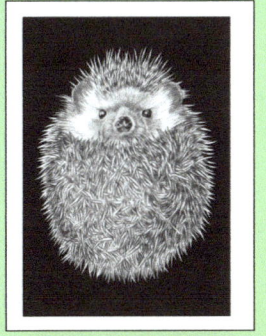
African Pygmy Hedgehog 2

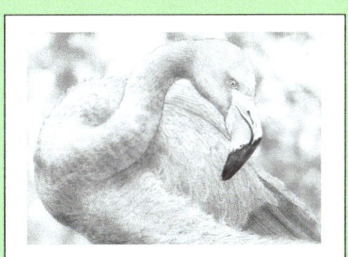
Greater Flamingo 5

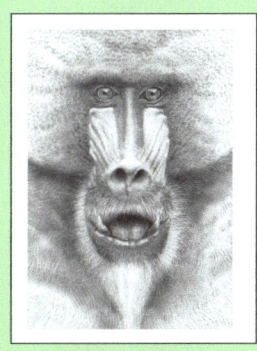
Mandrill 8

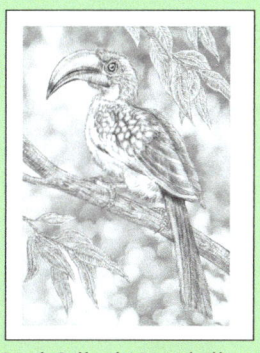
Red-Billed Hornbill 11

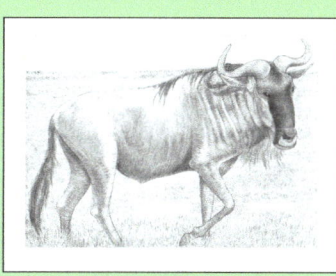
Wildebeest 14

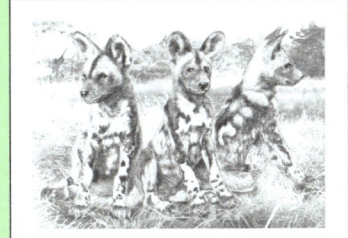
African Wild Dogs 3

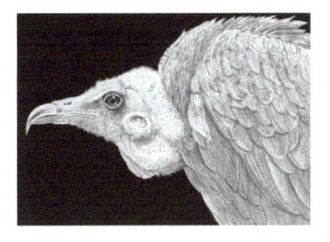
Hooded Vulture 6

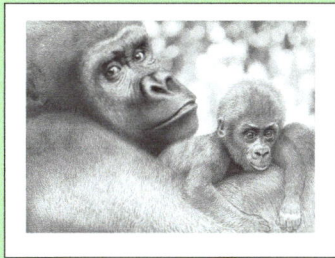
Mountain Gorillas 9

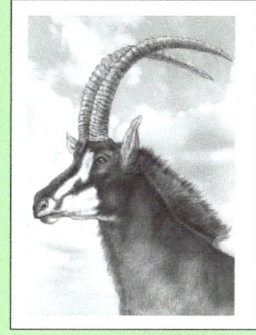
Sable Antelope 12

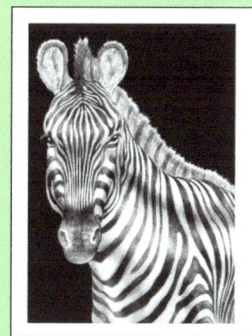
Zebra 15

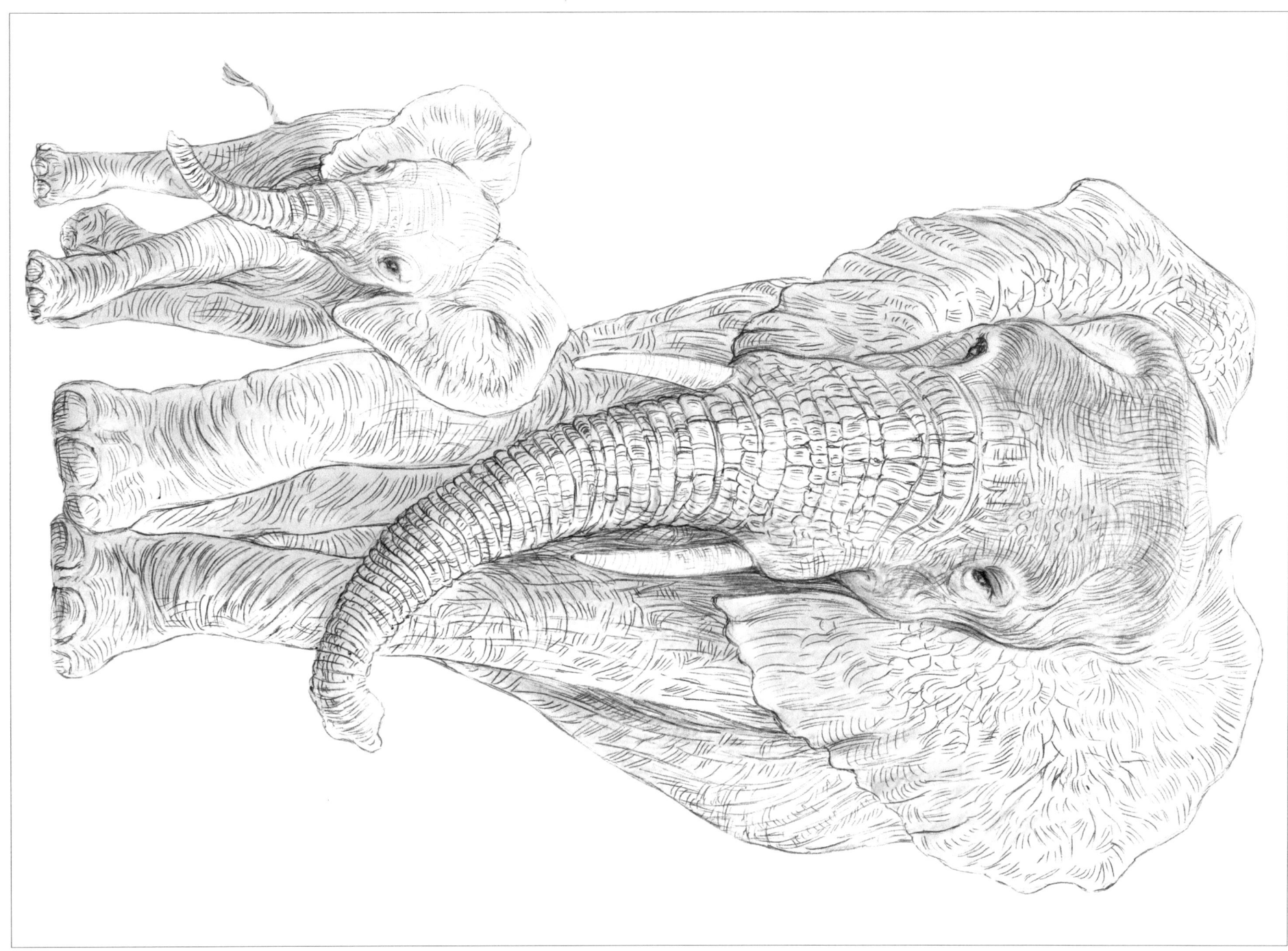

African Bush Elephants

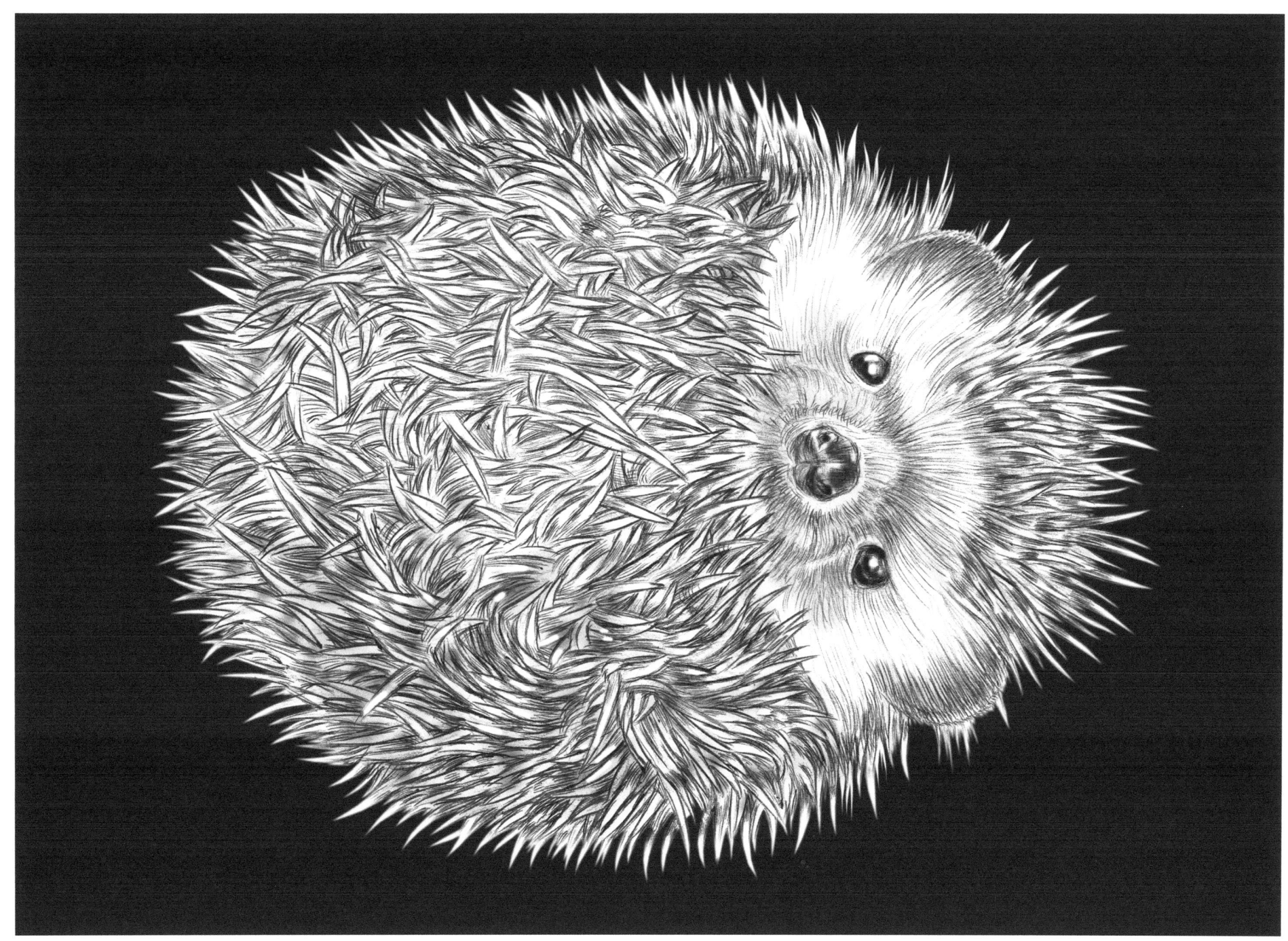

African Pygmy Hedgehog

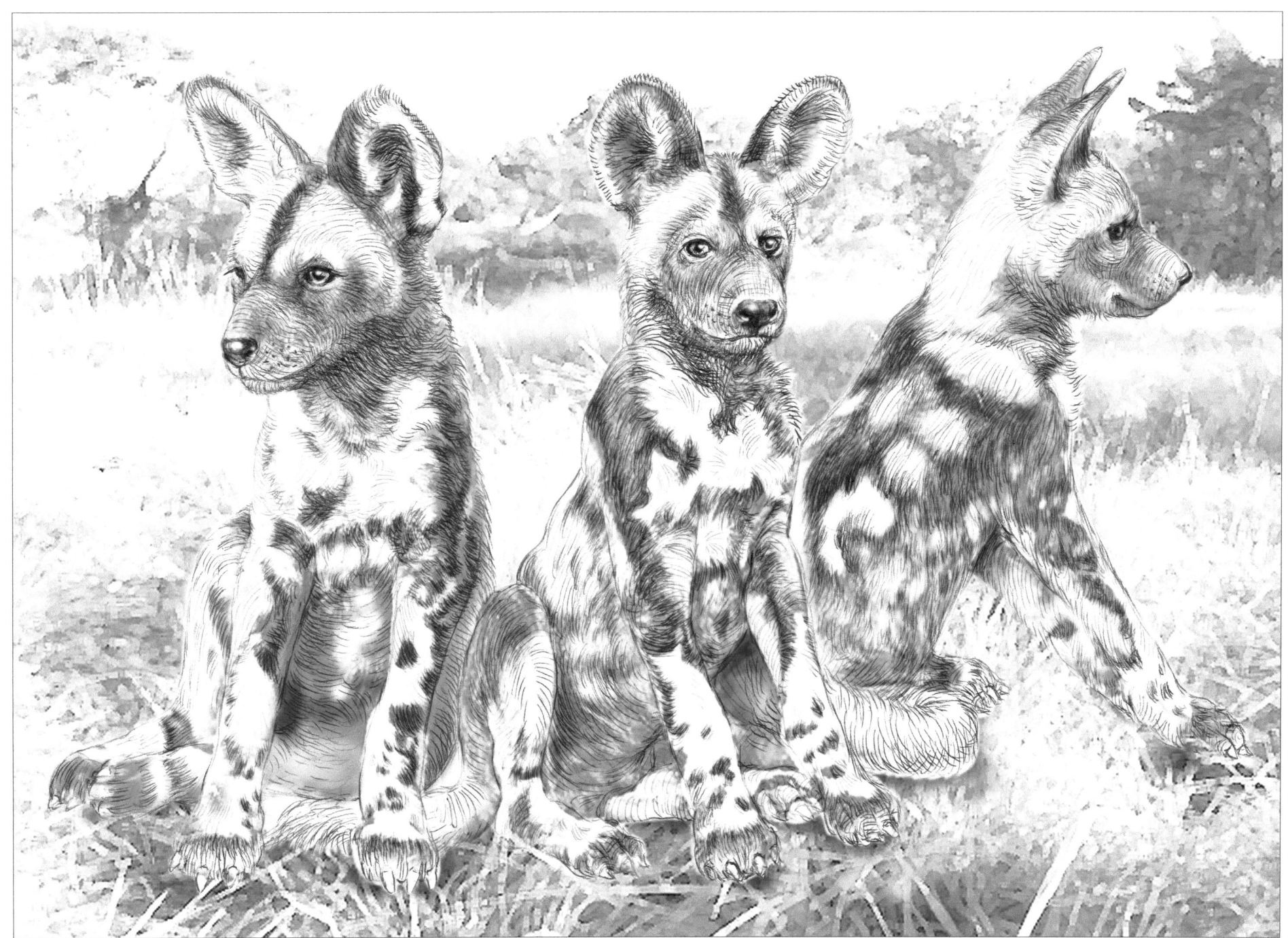

African Wild Dogs

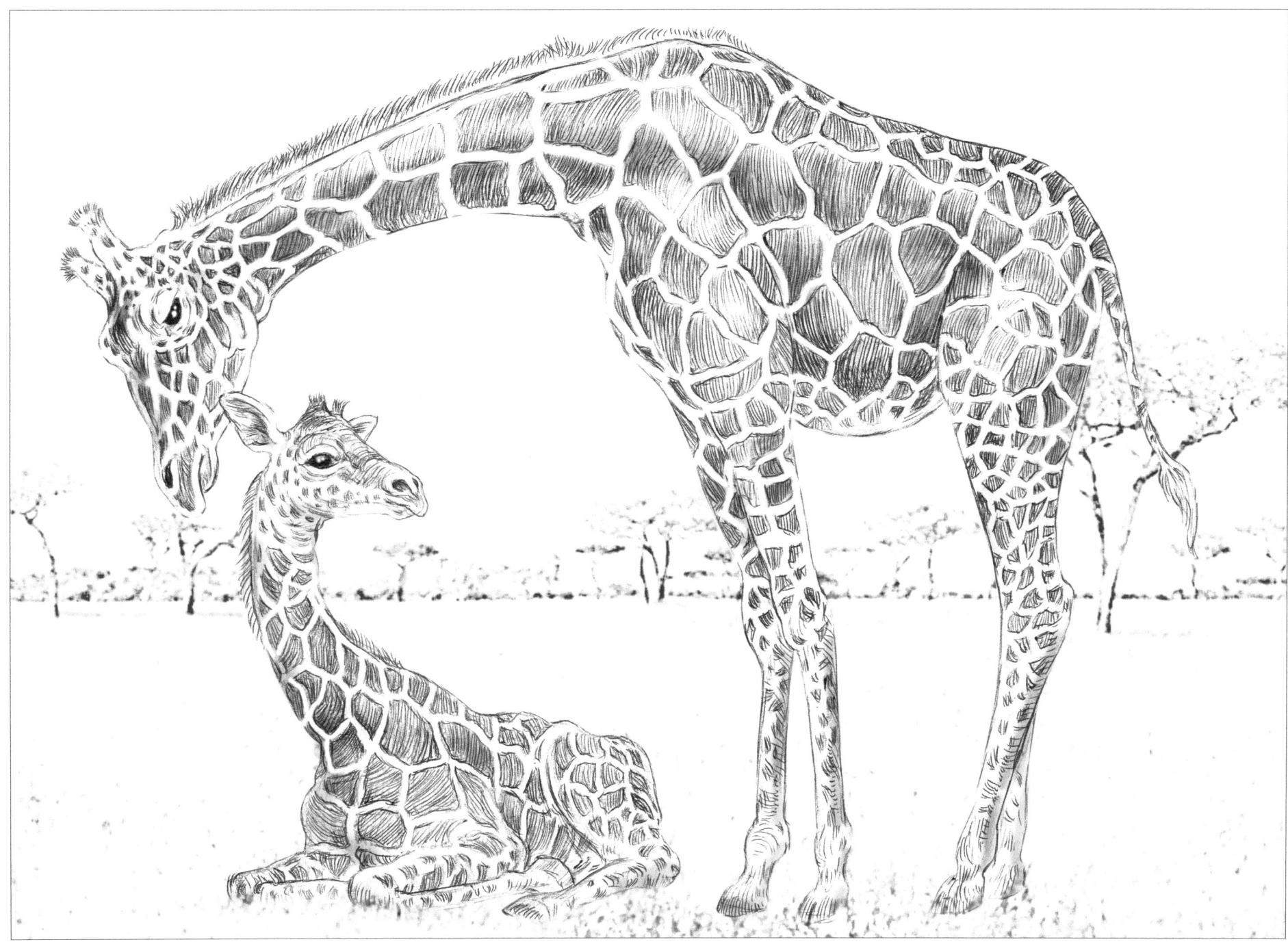

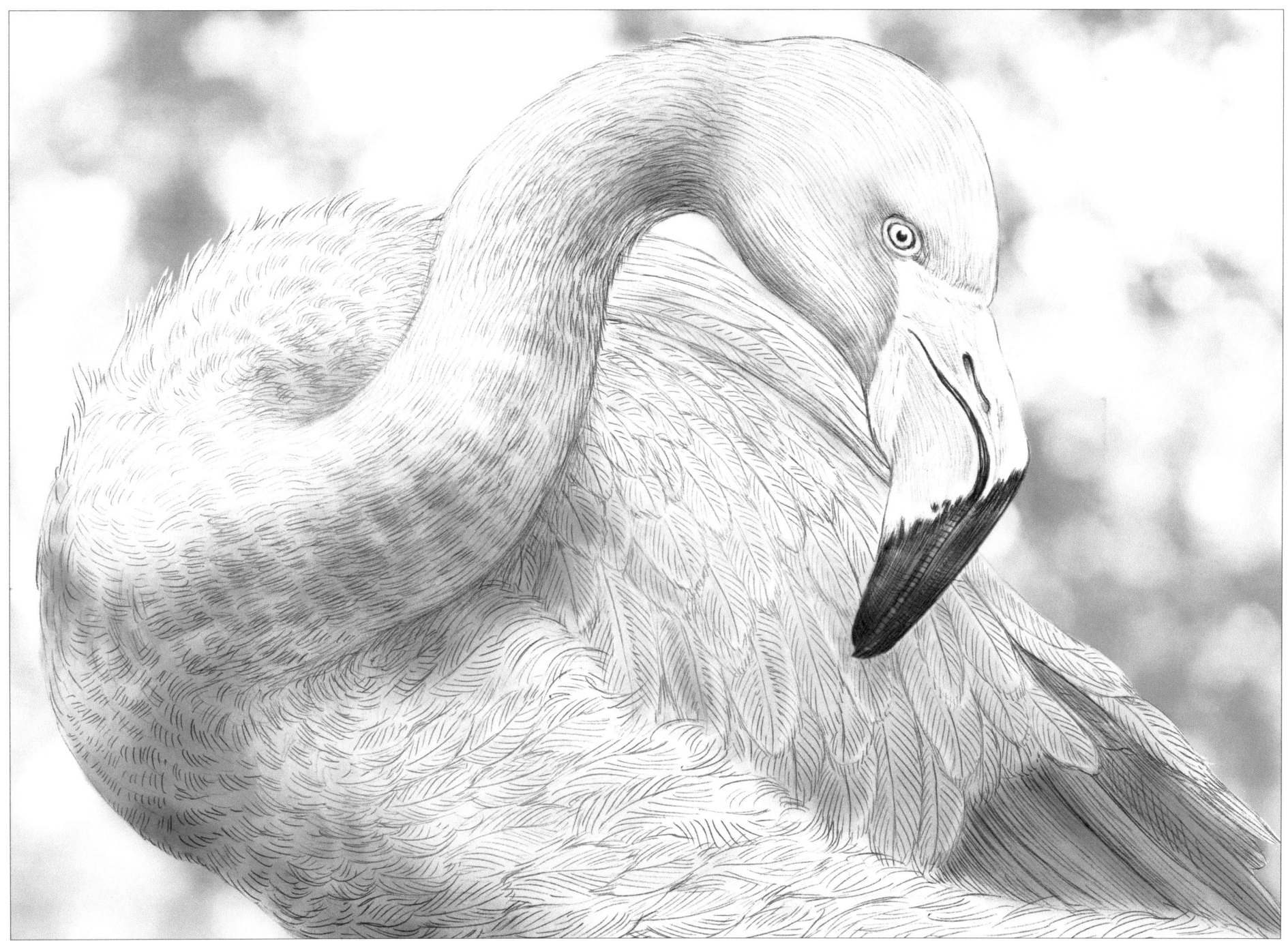

Greater Flamingo

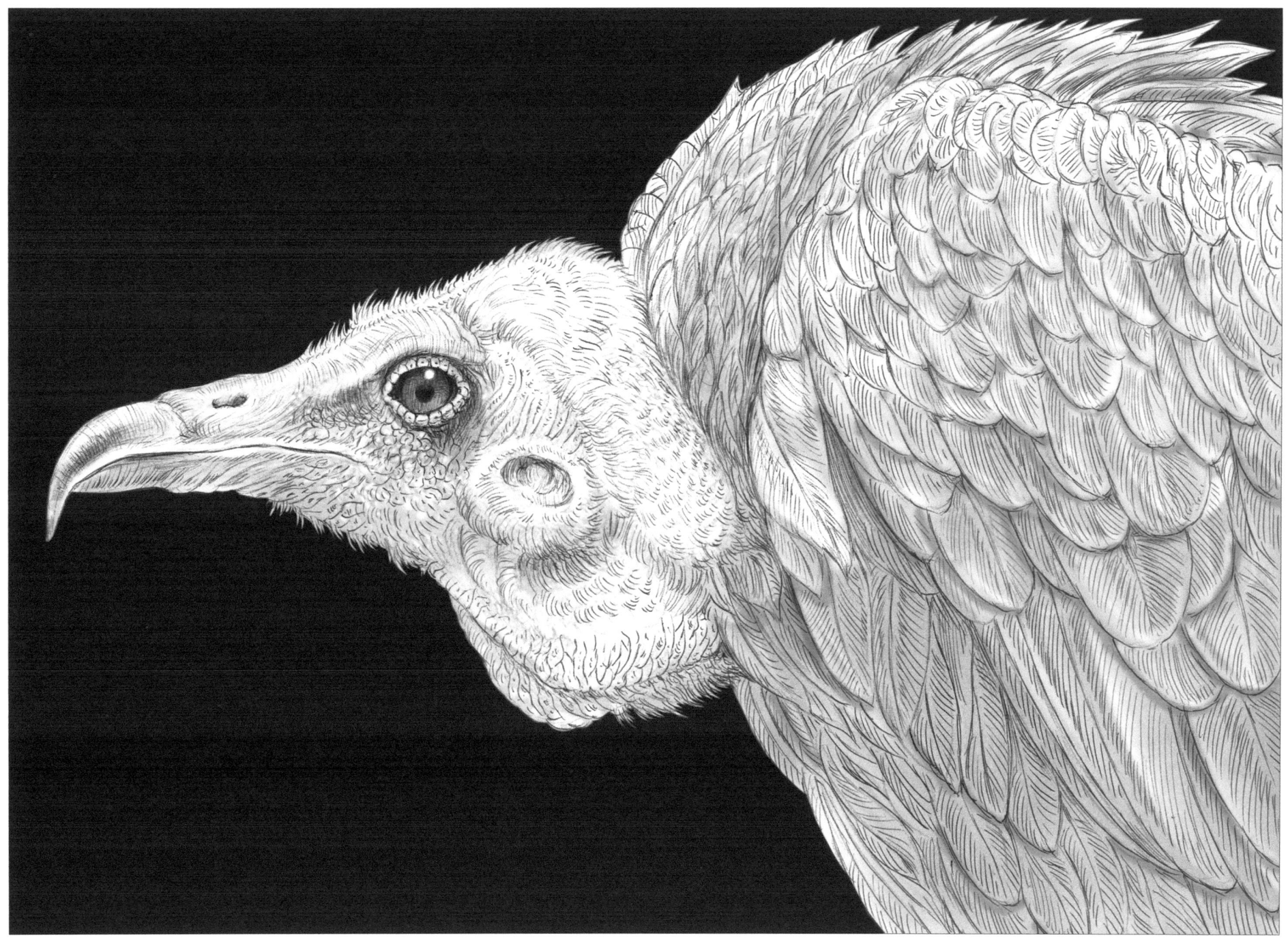

Hooded Vulture

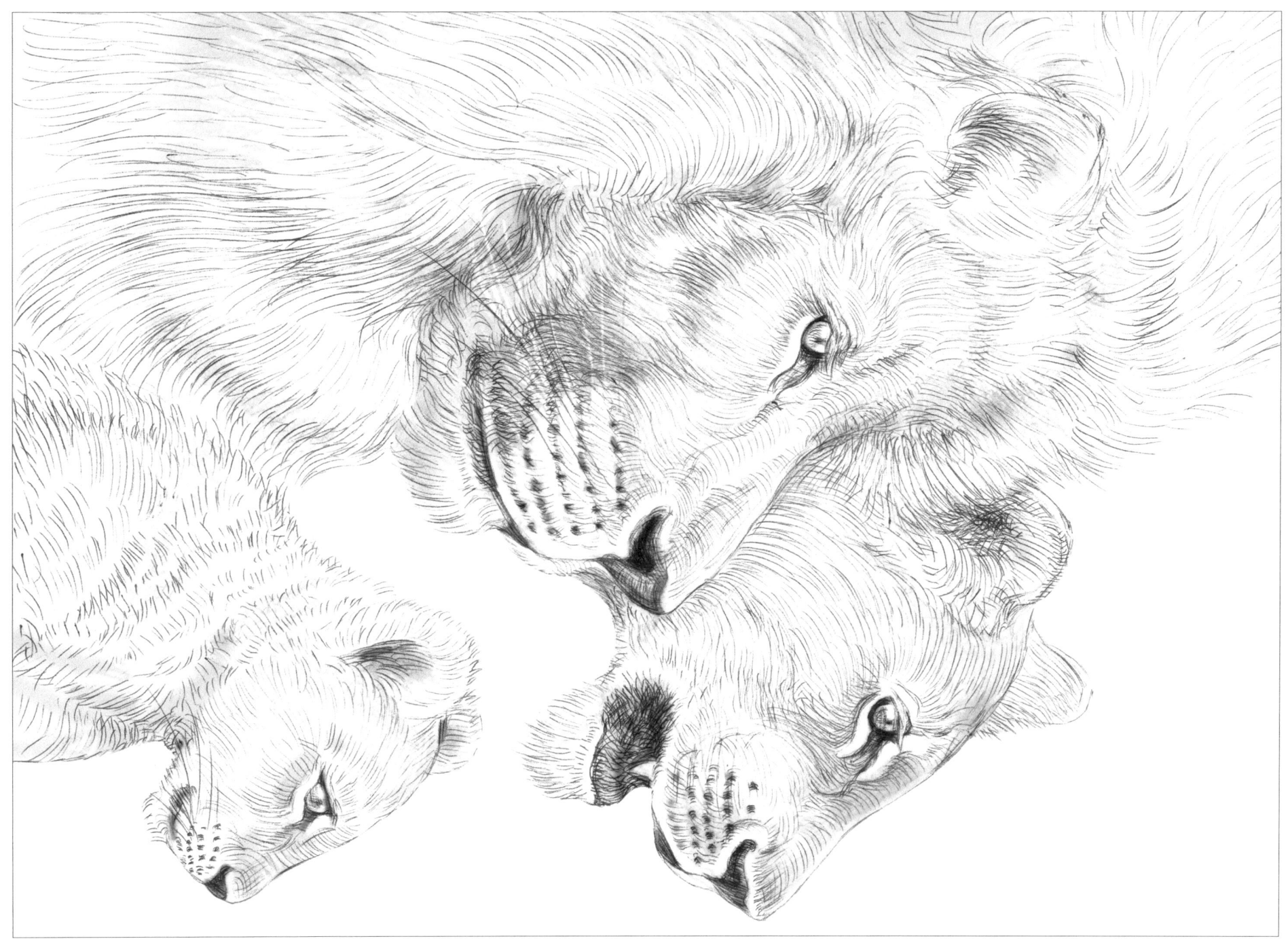

Lions

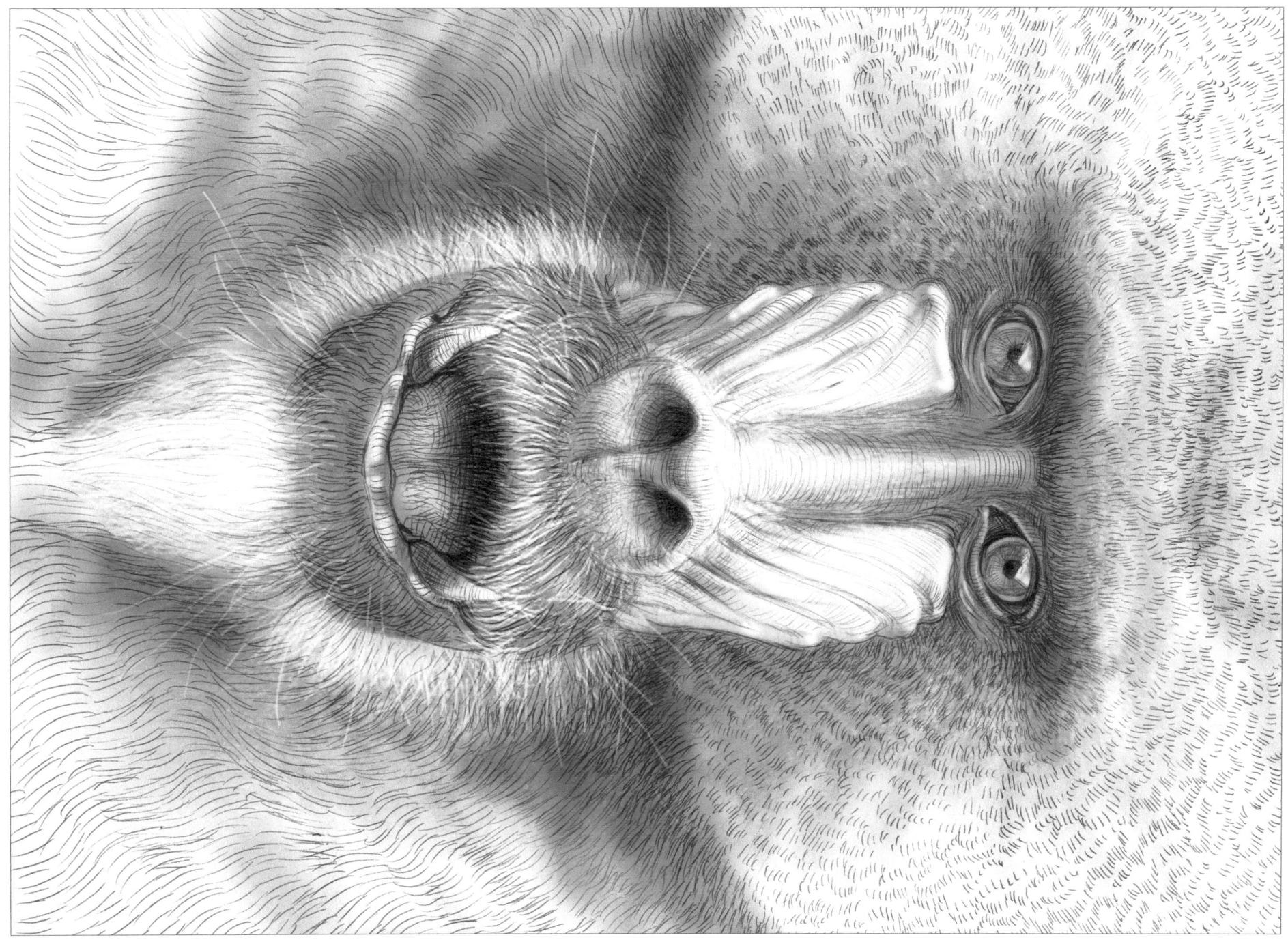

Mandrill

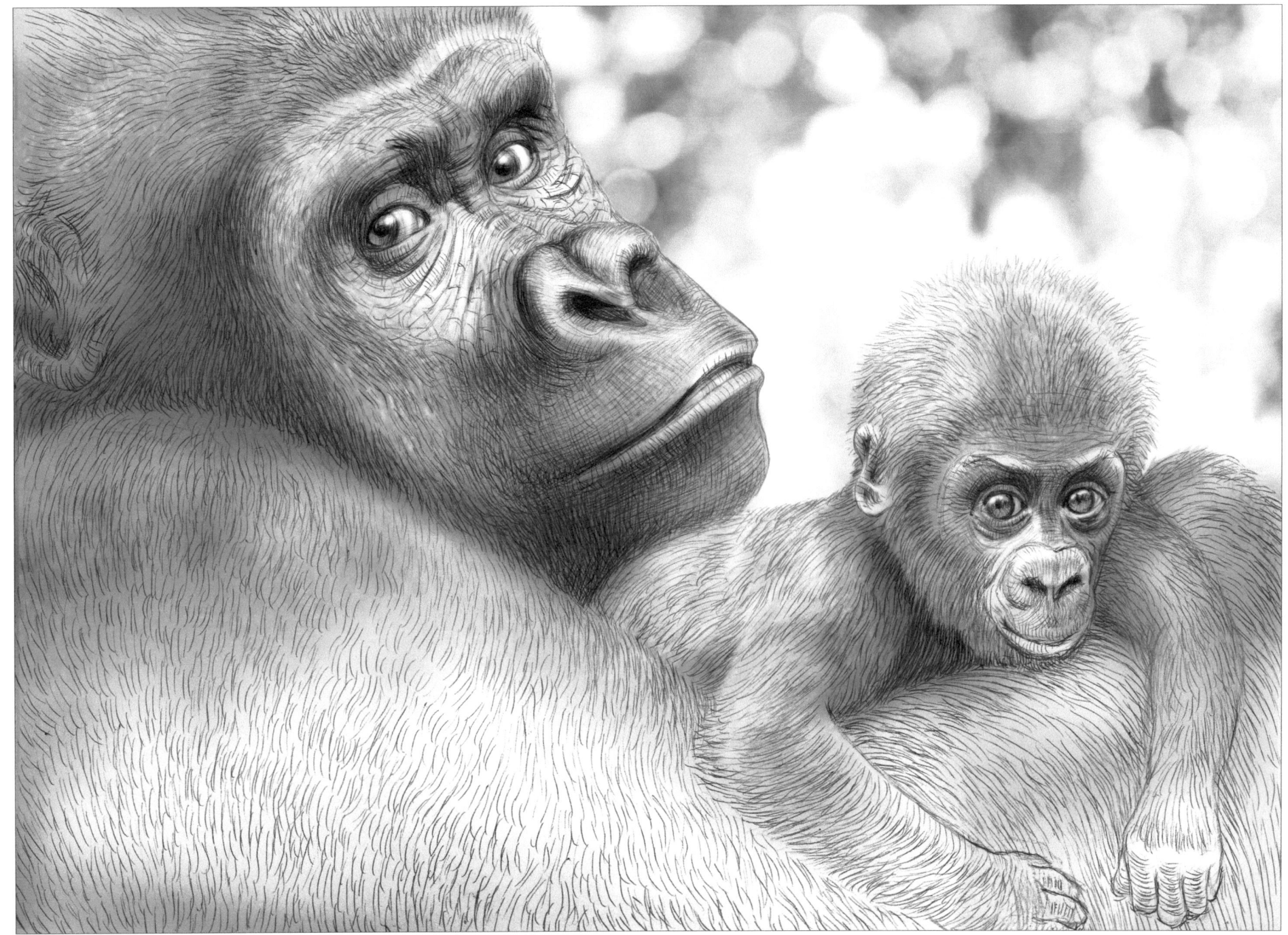

Mountain Gorillas

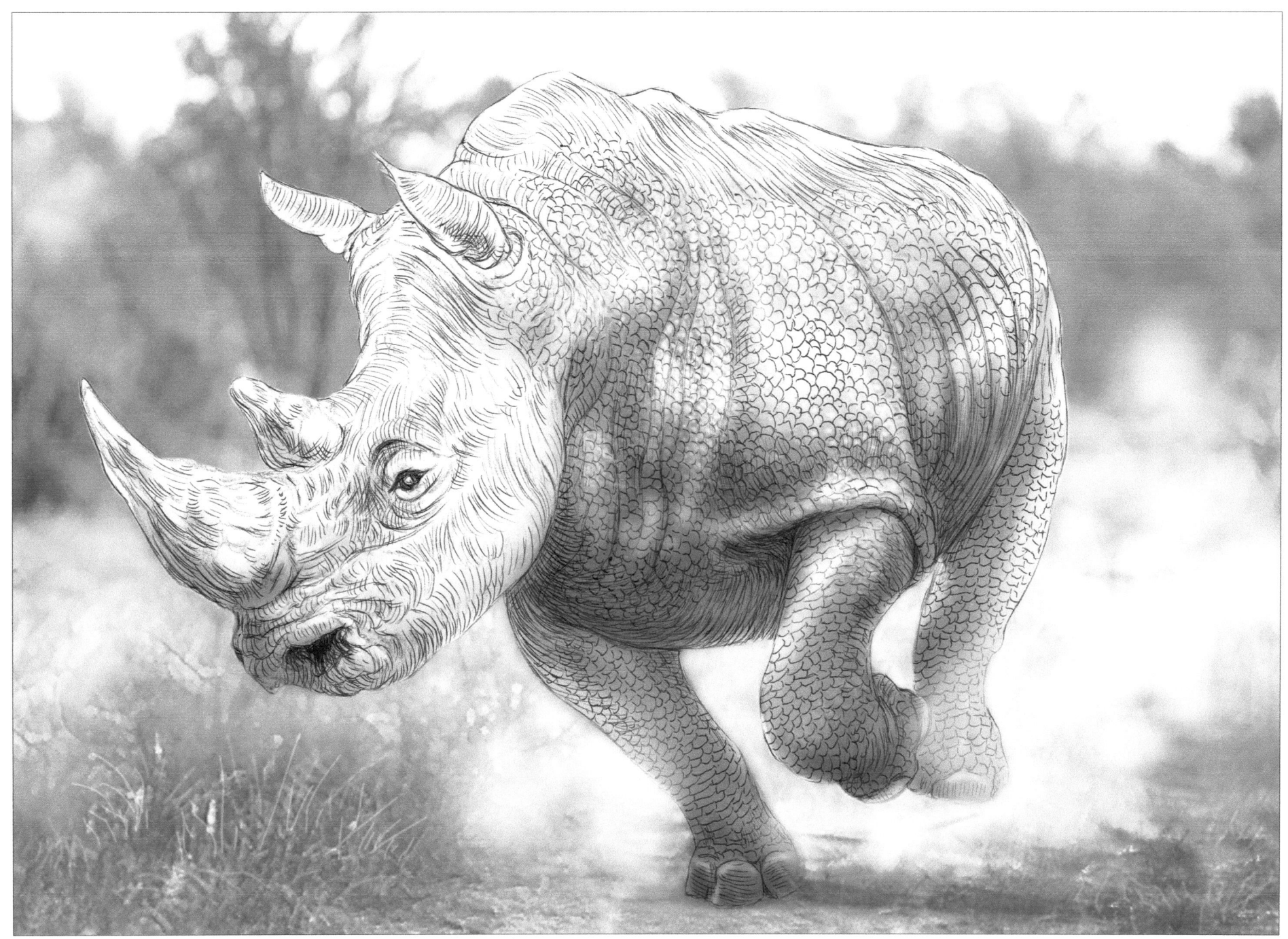

Northern White Rhinoceros

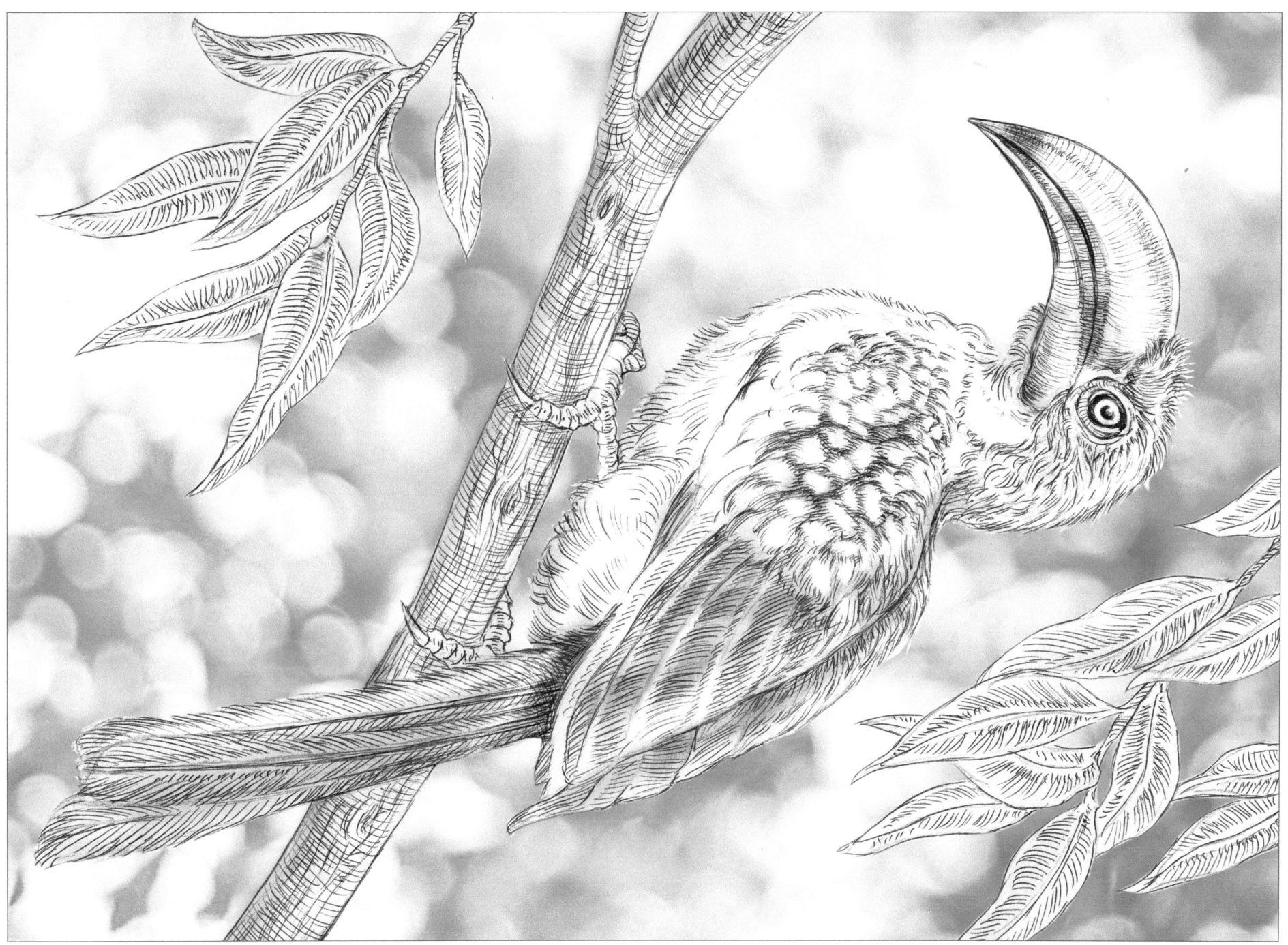

Red-Billed Hornbill

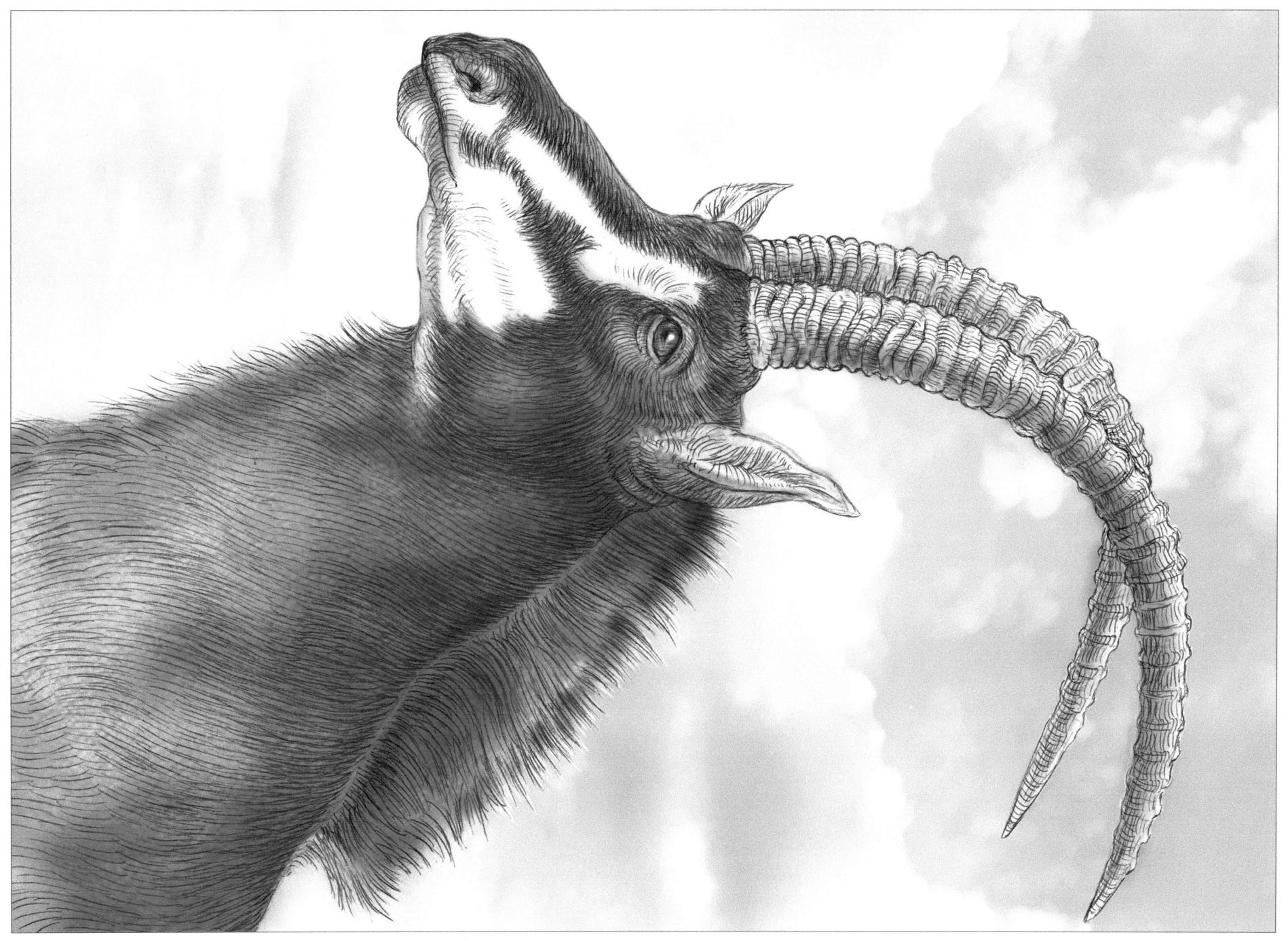
Sable Antelope

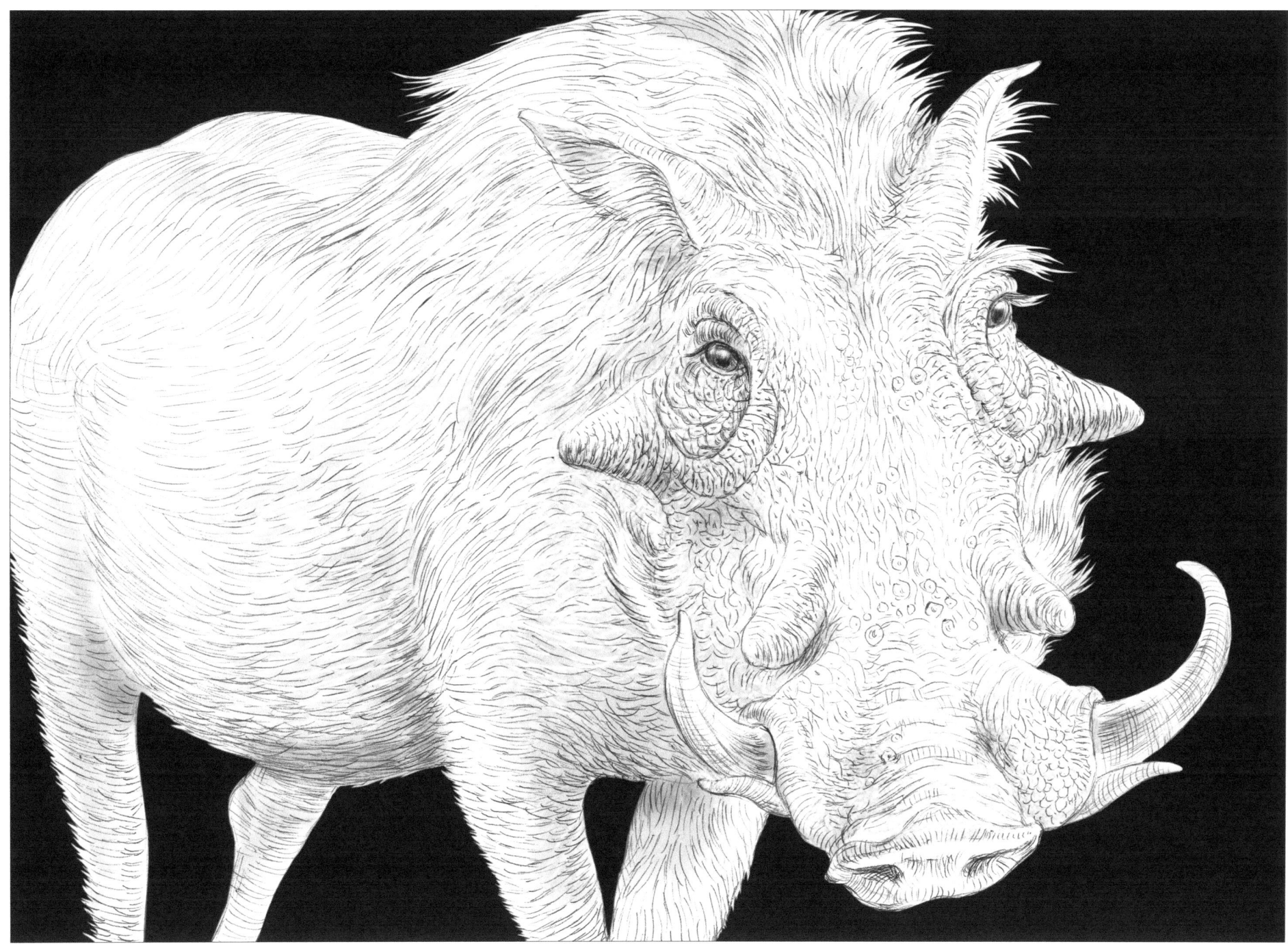

Warthog

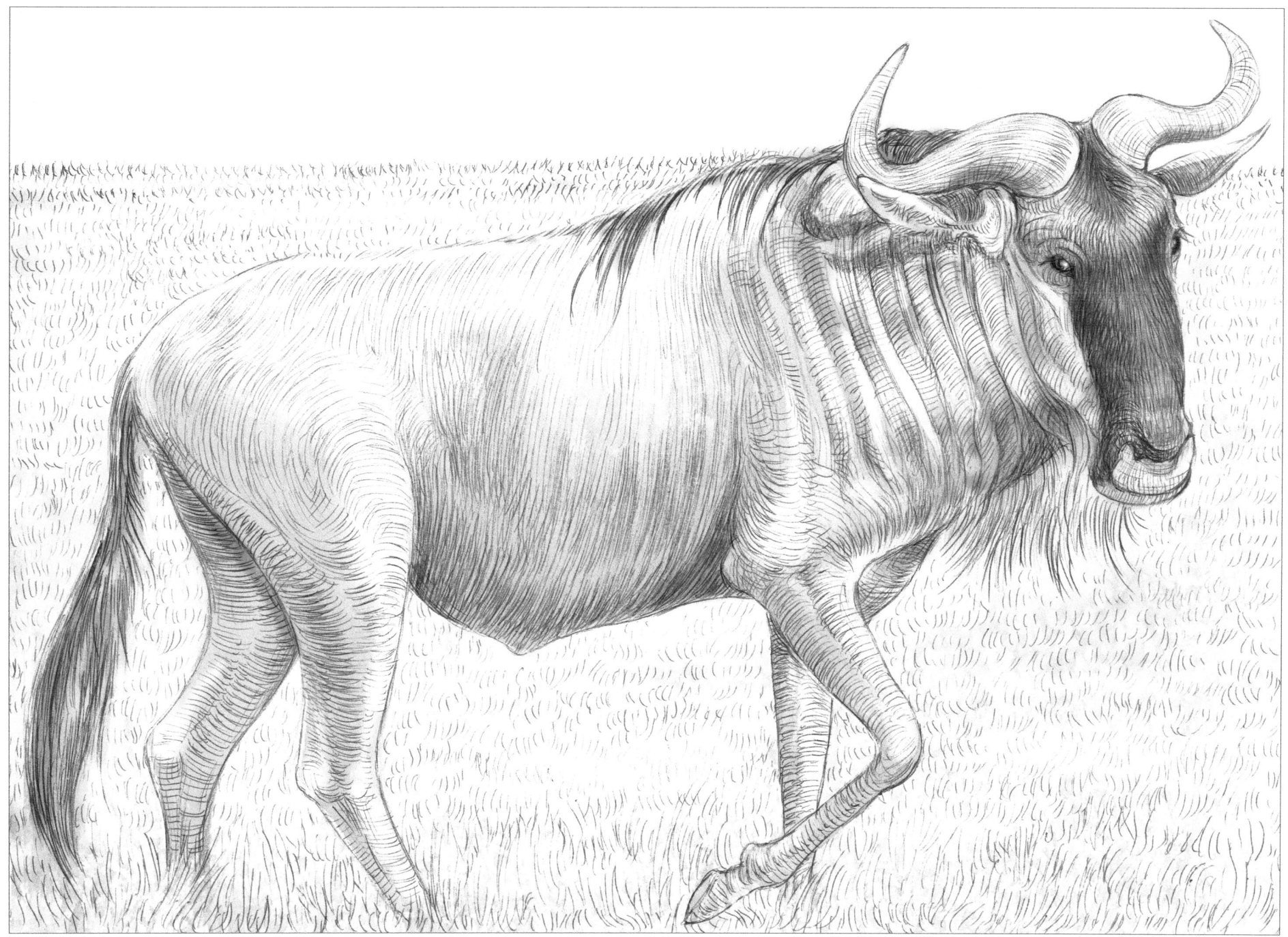

Wildebeest

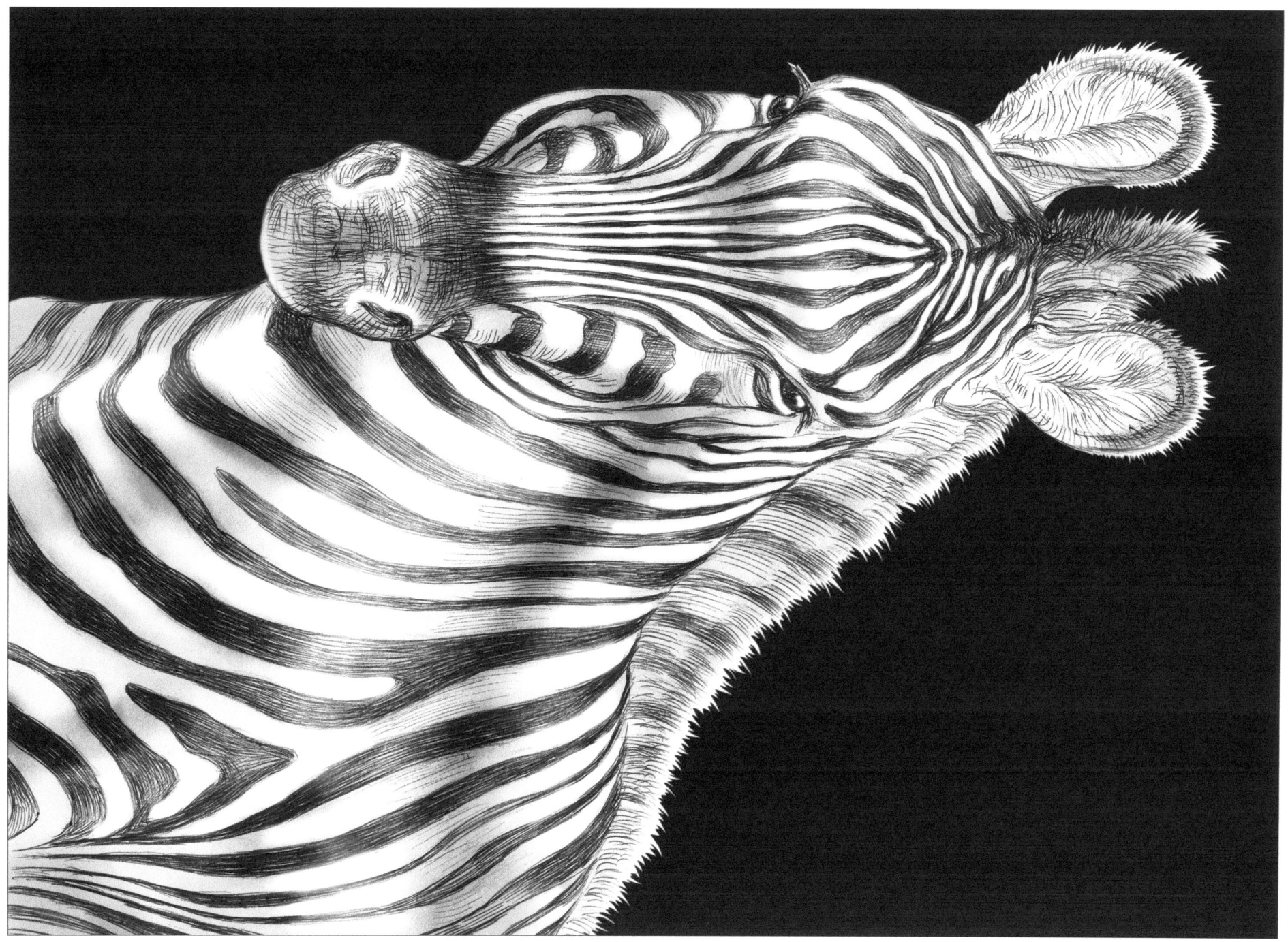

Zebra

Tim Jeffs is a New York City based artist and illustrator who has been creating dynamic artwork for over 25 years. Animals are a favorite subject matter of his, along with the complex and intricate details these creatures possess. *"The incredible diversity and complexity of animals has always intrigued me. They offer endless pleasure to look and marvel upon. In every drawing I try to capture the unique quality of each particular animal. I hope you enjoy my perspective, love and admiration of these incredible creatures."*

Visit my website for prints, digital coloring books and coloring lessons:
www.TimJeffsArt.com

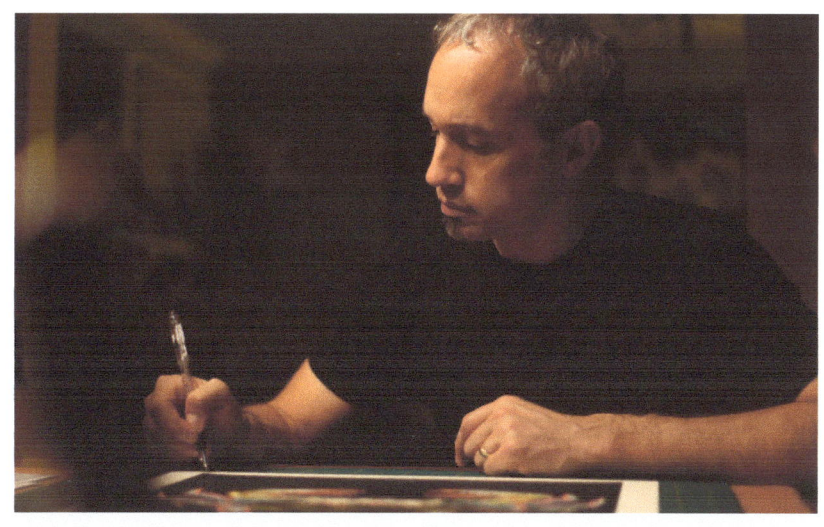

Discover the full line of Tim Jeffs' Published Coloring Books

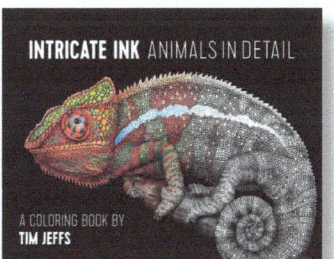 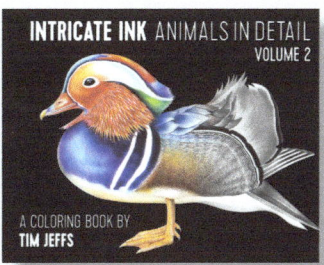 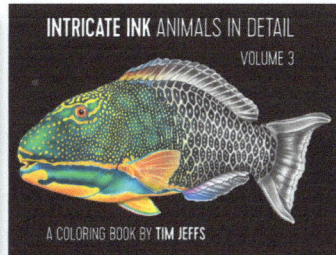 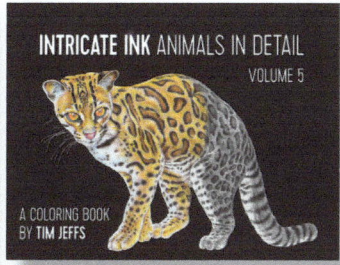 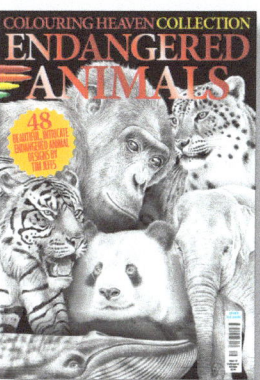

Intricate Ink Animals In Detail Volume 1, 2 3 and 5, and Intricate Animal Drawings Volume 1 and 2 are available at:
Amazon.com
Bookdepository.com

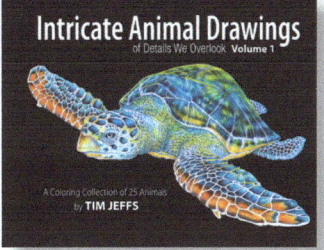 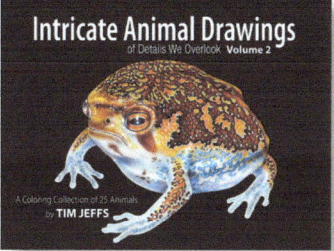

Colouring Heaven Collection Endangered Animals
Available at: Colouringheaven.com

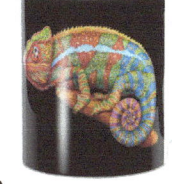

Discover Tim Jeffs' Merchandise

Etsy Shop
www.etsy.com/shop/TimJeffsArt

Society6 Shop
www.society6.com/TimJeffsArt

Redbubble Shop
TimJeffsArt.redbubble.com

TeePublic Shop
https://www.teepublic.com/user/tim-jeffs-art

Discover the full line of Tim Jeffs Digital Coloring Books and Lessons at www.timjeffsart.com

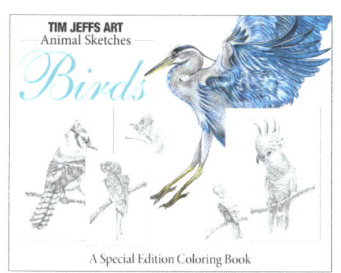 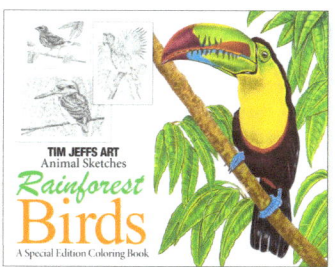 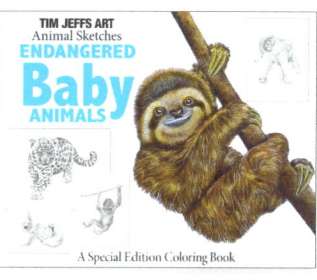 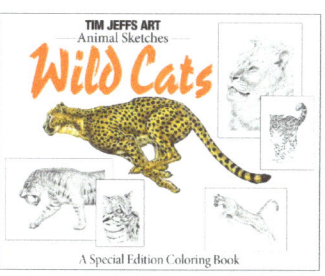 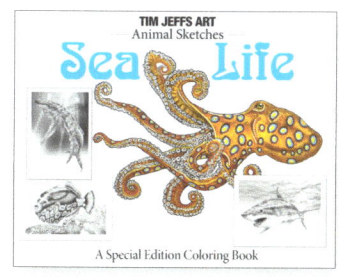
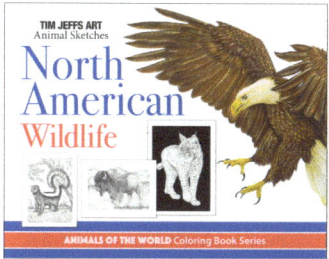 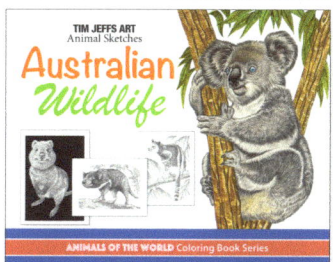 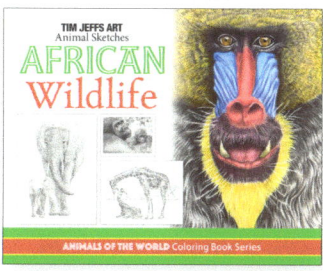 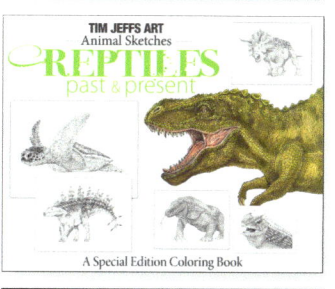 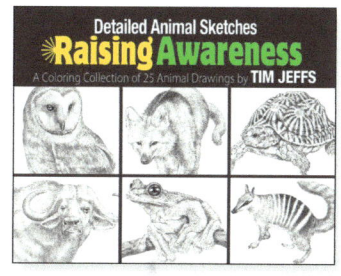
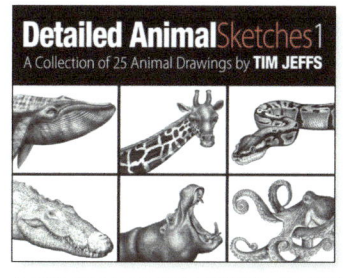 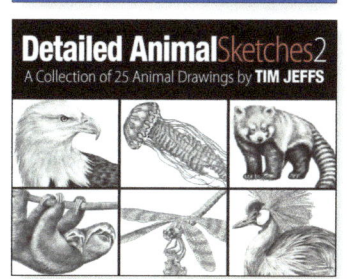 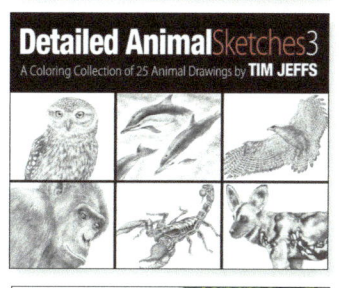 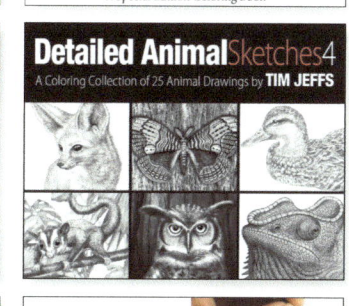 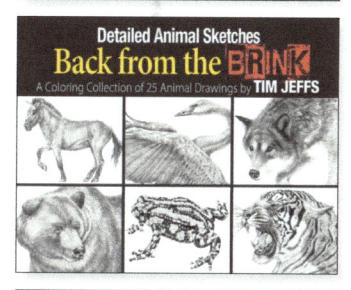
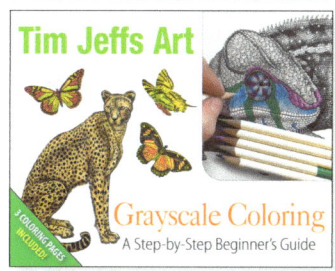 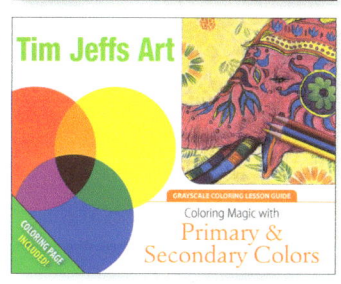 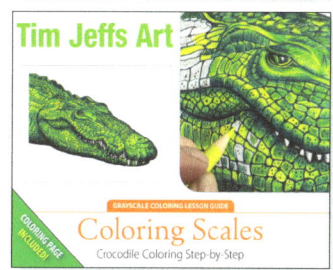 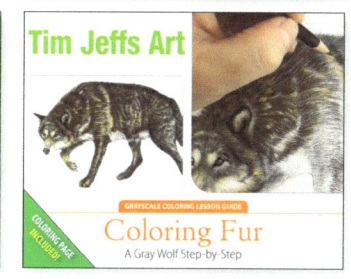 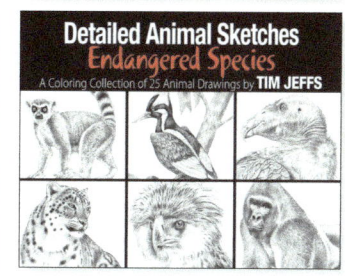
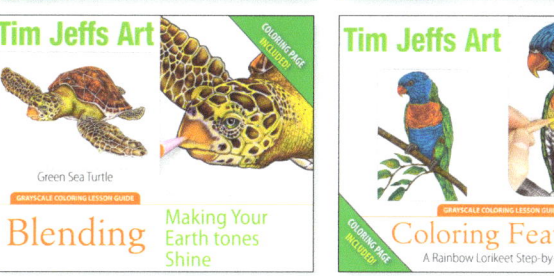 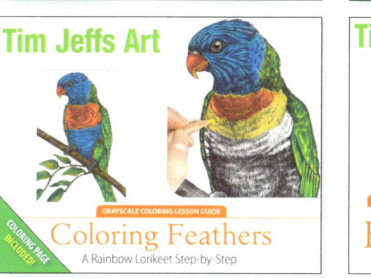 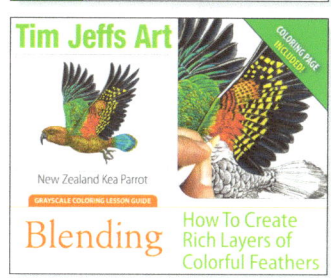 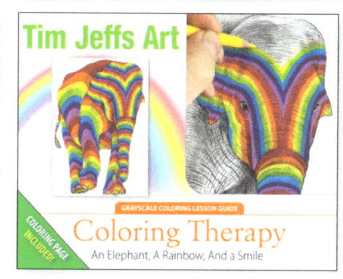

TIM JEFFS ART Online Resources

Share Your Creativity with the World!

Join the ever-expanding coloring group of animal lovers who inspire each other through their colorings of the animals from Tim's books and lessons. With thousands of members from all around the world, Tim's Facebook group "Intricate Ink Coloring Group" is a creative and safe space where everyone is welcome. Jo Warren, the groups all-inspiring administrator will welcome you in with open arms and is there to encourage everyone to just have fun no matter your coloring skill level. Come join, we can't wait to have you as a member! Join Tim's Facebook Coloring Group at:

www.facebook.com/groups/intricateink

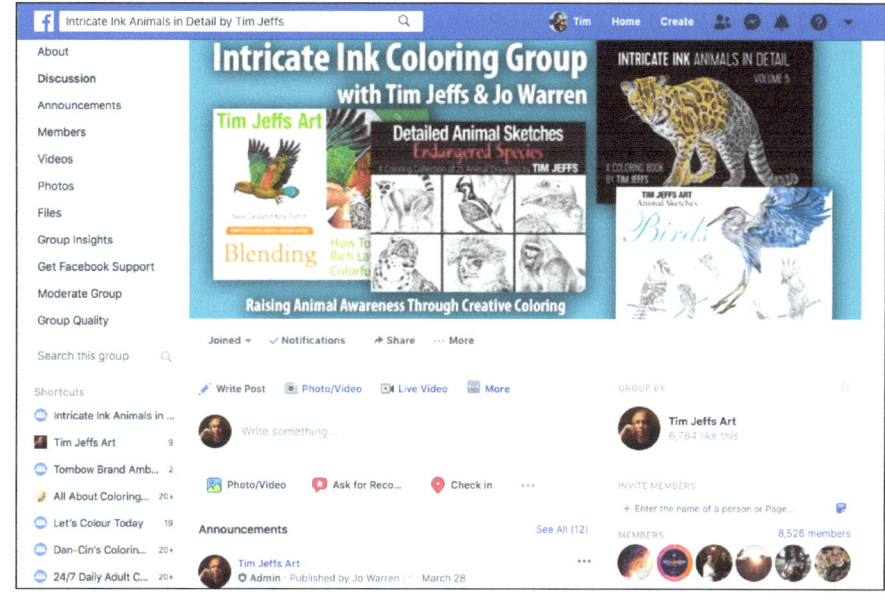

Visit the Home of Tim Jeffs Art

TimJeffsArt.com is my home on the web where I display all of my work and various projects. I hope you can stop by for a visit! You'll find my new shop where signed and unsigned prints of all of my animal drawings are available to purchase, along with the complete library of my digital download coloring books and grayscale coloring lessons. In the conservation section, you can see the projects that I am very proud of. Using my art to preserve wildlife is so important to me.

www.TimJeffsArt.com

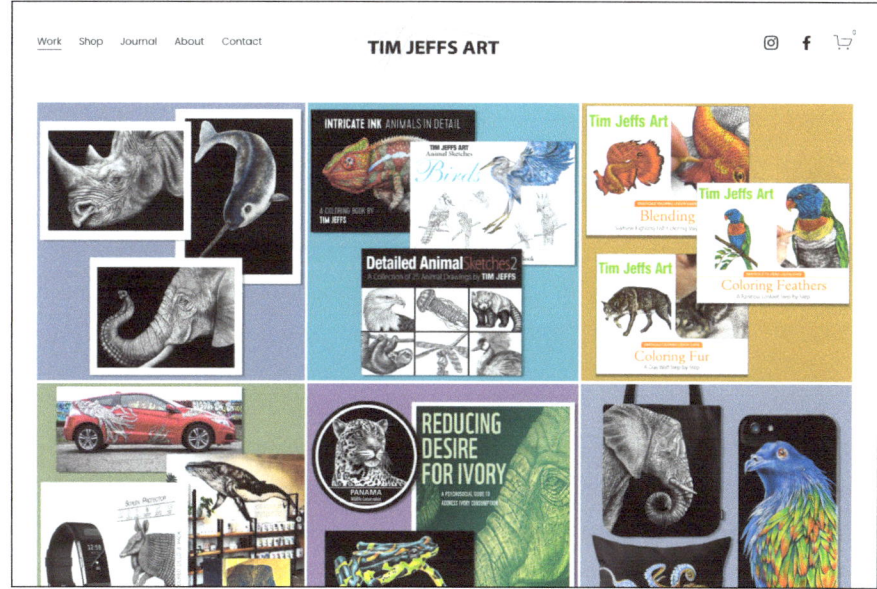